FIESTA!

PERU

GROLIER EDUCATIONAL

SHERMAN TURNPIKE, DANBURY, CONNECTICUT 06816

Published 1997 by Grolier Educational
Sherman Turnpike, Danbury, Connecticut.
Copyright © 1997 Marshall Cavendish Limited.

Set ISBN : 0-7172-9099-9
Volume ISBN : 0-7172-9106-5

Library of Congress Cataloging-in-Publication Data
Peru.
p.cm. -- (Fiesta!)
Includes index.
Summary: Discusses the festivals of this South American country and how its songs, recipes, and traditions
reflect the culture of the people.
ISBN 0-7172-9106-5
1. Peru -- Social life and customs -- Juvenile literature. 2. Peru -- Religious life and customs-- Juvenile literature.
[1. Festivals -- Peru. 2. Peru -- Holidays. 3. Peru -- Social life and customs.]
I. Grolier Educational (Firm) II. Series: Fiesta! (Danbury, Conn.)
F3410.P44 1997
985--DC21
97-16746
CIP
AC

Marshall Cavendish Limited
Editorial staff
Editorial Director: Ellen Dupont
Series Designer: Joyce Mason
Crafts devised and created by Susan Moxley
Music arrangements by Harry Boteler
Photographs by Bruce Mackie
Subeditors: Susan Janes, Judy Fovargue
Production: Craig Chubb

For this volume
Editor: Charles Phillips
Designer: Melissa Stokes
Consultant: Lucy Davies
Editorial Assistant: Lorien Kite

Printed in Italy

Adult supervision advised for all crafts and recipes
particularly those involving sharp instruments and heat.

CONTENTS

PERU:

In northwestern South America Peru was home to the Incas before being conquered by the Spanish in the 1500s.

Andes

Pacific Ocean

▼ **Ruins** of the Inca city of Macchu Picchu lie high in the mountains about 50 miles from Cuzco.

◀ **Inca knives** are today made as good luck tokens. In Inca times priests used knives like this in their ceremonies.

▼ **Corn** is an important food. It is grown in the highlands of central Peru. People also make drinks out of corn.

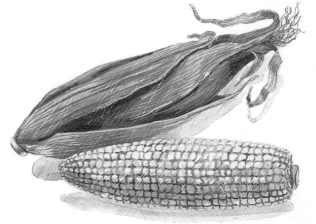

Colombia

ador

Brazil

Ucayali

Huallaga

Peru

Urubamba

LIMA

Cuzco

Bolivia

Puno

Lake Titicaca

Chile

▼ **Lima** is the capital of Peru. This sandy colored cathedral lies on one side of the Plaza de Armas in the city. Lima was built by Francisco Pizarro, a Spanish leader who conquered Peru in the 1500s.

5

RELIGIONS

Most Peruvians are Christians. But some of them still believe in parts of the Incas' religion. The Incas ruled Peru before the Spanish conquered the country in the 1500s.

CHRISTIANITY in Peru has a special flavor. Catholicism is the most popular form of Christianity in the country. There are many Catholic churches. Most Peruvian festivals are on Catholic holy days. But the beliefs and customs of the Incas are also important. Many Catholic festivals are tied to ancient Inca ceremonies. At Corpus Christi, a Catholic feast in June, people in Cuzco march

Even small mountain villages usually have their own Catholic churches. But people remember the old Inca customs, too.

Martin de Porres was born in the Peruvian capital Lima in 1579 and lived as a monk. He was made a saint many years later.

in procession with large statues of saints. This custom came from an Inca festival that was held each year. The festival marked the year's first sighting of the Pleiades constellation – a group of stars – in the night sky. The Inca Indians used to carry images of their dead leaders in this festival. Cuzco was their capital city. Today the Catholic festival is still quite closely based on the original Inca ceremonies.

The Incas believed that mountains have spirits, or *apus*. They honored the apus and made offerings to them.

6

When mountain snows melt, the waters flow down to feed crops in the hills below. This may be one reason why the Incas honored mountain apus. They also believed that on mountains they could be close to people who had died – their fathers, mothers, and all those who had come before them. They believed that when people died, they became part of the universe. First they went up to the sky, then they came down to "Pachamama," Mother Earth. The Incas looked to the stars for help when making decisions. On mountain tops they could be close to the stars. The festival of Qoyllur Rit'i in May or June is based on the old Inca beliefs. People make a religious journey to honor the mountain apus. Today Qoyllur Rit'i also has a Christian element. Some come to worship the Lord of Qoyllur Rit'i, a vision of Jesus.

GREETINGS FROM **PERU!**

Peru is the third largest country in South America. Only Brazil and Argentina are bigger. Most of Peru's cities sit on a narrow strip of flat land along the coast of the Pacific Ocean. Behind lies a wide mountainous area called the *sierra*. Many Peruvians live in small villages in the sierra. Their lives are very hard. They have to grow enough food to survive for the whole year. Peruvians speak Spanish (right), or Quechua, which is based on the language spoken by the Incas.

How do you say...

Hello

Hola

Goodbye

Adiós

Thank you

Gracias

Peace

Paz

VIRGIN OF CANDELARIA

Dancers fill the streets of Puno, in southern Peru, for several days in February. They perform folk dances in colorful costumes.

The sound of drums, violins, trumpets, flutes, and panpipes fills the town of Puno during this festival. Crowds gather to listen and to watch the dancers.

The party goes on for ten days. The main event is the Catholic festival of Candlemas, Candelaria in Spanish, which is on February 2. It marks the day when the baby Jesus was taken to the Temple in Jerusalem – the center of the Jewish religion.

A statue of Mary, the mother of Jesus, is carried through the streets on Candlemas

The diablada, or devil dance, thrills the crowds at the festival. Dancers dress as devils – or wicked spirits. The dance goes back to the time before Peru was Christian.

day. People throw wild flowers at the statue. In one square, called the Plaza de Armas, four altars are built. An altar is a table

Bands of musicians come from miles around to play at the festival. They have a vast range of panpipes. The biggest is almost as tall as a man. It plays very low notes.

different costumes. Some wear shepherds' outfits, some make themselves look like frightening animals. Others dress up like the *conquistadors*, the Spanish settlers who conquered Peru in the 1500s. They perform a comic dance to make fun of the Spanish.

The most exciting of all are the devil dancers. These have masks and costumes made from very costly materials like silk and velvet and decorated with jewels and gold and silver studs.

on which offerings are made to God. These altars are decorated in honor of Mary.

At the end of the parade the image of Mary is put back in the Church of San Juan, where it is kept. On the other days of the festival dancers stop just outside the church to perform.

The groups of dancers wear many

Devil masks dominate this Peruvian vision of hell (below, left). The right-hand scene shows the birth of Jesus Christ. The figures have been arranged inside a dried gourd.

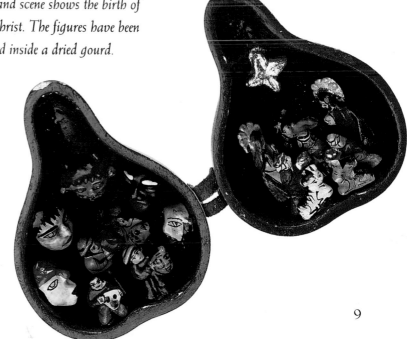

HOLY WEEK

Peruvians celebrate the Christian festival of Easter for a whole week. They take part in religious processions.

Easter Day is the most important day in the whole year for Christians. They believe that Jesus Christ came back to life after He had been dead for three days. Easter Day, a Sunday, is the time when Christians celebrate Jesus's "resurrection" – His coming back to life from death.

Peruvians start their Easter party on the Monday before Easter Day. In Cuzco, eastern Peru, people carry a statue of Jesus in a long procession through the streets on this day.

Cuzco suffers from earthquakes. A very bad one hit the city in 1650, on March 31. People believe that the statue of Jesus saved Cuzco from being destroyed on that day. They call it "Our Lord of the Earthquakes." They carry the statue to the Cathedral and pray that Jesus will save them from any more earthquakes.

Dancing, feasting, and drinking are a major part of Holy Week parties. Spicy snacks and sweets like

Catholic churches in Peru are often richly decorated. Ornate images made of metals and semiprecious stones are hung on the walls. Designs include Christian symbols such as the Crucifix and the Virgin.

besitos are sold on the streets. People drink *chicha*, a beer brewed using corn.

In Ayacucho, close to Cuzco, artists make images on the ground using flowers. People then march through the flower carpets and break up the images with their feet.

Judas, one of Jesus's friends, cheated Jesus. He gave Jesus to his enemies. On Good Friday, the day when Jesus died, images of Judas are hung up and burned in many

BESITOS ("LITTLE KISSES")

MAKES ABOUT 20
1 can (14 oz) sweetened condensed milk
About 3½ cups shredded coconut

1 Pour sweetened condensed milk into large mixing bowl.
2 Add 3½ cups shredded coconut. Stir until mixture becomes thick. If mixture is not thick, stir in a little more coconut.
3 Cover bowl with plastic wrap. Put in refrigerator until mixture becomes stiff enough to hold its shape when molded.
4 Using your hands, roll into small balls. Place the balls on a plate. If not serving at once, cover and chill.

People dress up in all their finest clothes for the outdoor celebrations during Holy Week. Parties go on for hours. Food is on sale at street stands for those who grow hungry.

Peruvian towns. On the night before Good Friday prayers go on all night in Ayacucho.

Many Peruvian Catholics believe that in the days between Good Friday and Easter Sunday God will not see what they do because Jesus is dead. It is a chance for them to break rules and misbehave.

FIESTA DEL CRUZ

On May 3 people all over Peru celebrate the festival of the crosses, a mixture of Christianity and old Inca beliefs. It marks the end of the rainy season.

Some dancers at the Fiesta del Cruz look very like acrobats. They leap through the air as they perform the famous dance of the scissors. Big crowds come to watch them.

Sometimes the dance is terrifying to see because the dancers go through the steps on the tall belltower of a local church. Children and people who are watching the scissors dance for the

The Fiesta del Cruz is tied to the farming year. It comes in the first dry month after the rains. People look forward to the crops they will harvest in the coming weeks.

The musicians and dancers often wear brightly colored knitted hats like these. The Fiesta del Cruz, like many other festivals, is a time for dressing up and showing off.

first time cry out in fear. But the dancers are surefooted. They finish the thrilling dance and climb down safely to the ground.

The Fiesta del Cruz is an old festival. Long before the Spanish arrived in the 1500s, the Peruvian Indians were holding this fiesta. It marks the first sighting of the Southern Cross – a group of stars – in the night sky. By watching the sky, the Indians

Bands come from far and wide to the Fiesta del Cruz parties. Each area sends its own band, and they compete in long musical contests. The musicians play drums, panpipes, violins, and brass instruments like the trumpet.

learned that they saw the Southern Cross each year at the same time. It usually came, they realized, just when the rainy season had finished. It is an important part of the year for the Indians.

Many Peruvians farm hard, difficult mountain land. They need a good harvest to survive. May is when they harvest their potatoes. June is the usual month for the corn harvest. The Fiesta del Cruz is a kind of harvest festival. The people hope for bumper crops to see them through the year ahead.

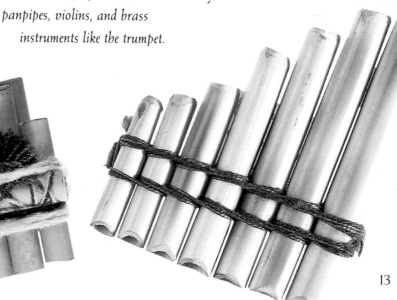

MAKE YOUR OWN CLAY MUSICIANS

Groups of clay figures are popular in Peru. Sometimes they show a line of musicians or men and women talking. Some groups have holes in their heads and double as a row of musical pipes.

YOU WILL NEED
Air-drying clay
Knife or sharp object to make scoring marks
Poster paints

1 Roll clay into sausage shapes about 3 inches long. Stick your thumb into one end to make a hollow sausage. Mold a face and hat on the figure. Make arms and instruments out of smaller clay pieces.

2 Scratch the surface of the clay where you want to stick the arms on the figure, then press together. Stick the figures together in the same way. When dry, paint brown, then use white to decorate.

When the Spanish conquered Peru, they brought their Christian customs with them. Roman Catholic religious festivals became mixed up with the Peruvian Indians' own ceremonies. Catholics honor the cross because it reminds them of the large, wooden cross to which Jesus Christ was nailed when He was crucified. Today the Christian cross plays a major part in the Fiesta del Cruz. People march in long processions, carrying large, heavy crosses between them. They also carry pictures of Jesus, of Mary, the mother of Jesus, and of Catholic saints.

The Fiesta del Cruz is a big party. As at other festivals, bands of musicians compete with one another. People dance to the music. In some parts of Peru villagers display *tablas de sarhua* at the Fiesta del Cruz. These are pictures painted on boards, which show scenes of life in the villages and within families.

PIRWALLA PIRWHA

Can-te-mos bai-le-mos to-dos pir-wa-lla pir-wa,

en es-ta pam-pa re-don-da, pir-wa-lla pir-wa,

to-dos bai-lan-do, pir-wa-lla pir-wa,

has-ta que yo di-ga, pir-wa-lla pir-wa,

el que no lo ha-ce pir-wa-lla pir-wa,

pa-ga la mul-ta, pir-wa-lla pir-wa.

Round dances are popular at festivals and parties. "Pirwalla pirwha" is a fun example. Appoint a "master" to shout out orders.

Let's sing, let's dance,
pirwalla pirwha,
In this vast grassland, p-pirwha,
Everybody dancing, p-pirwha,
Till I say "Stop", p-pirwha,
If you don't do it, p-pirwha,
You'll have to pay a fine,
pirwalla pirwha.

QOYLLUR RIT'I

In May or June pilgrims climb the slopes of the Ausangate peak in southern Peru. They dance, eat, and make music for three days.

People who live in villages high in the Andes have been traveling to the mountains of Qoyllur Rit'i and Ausangate for many years. It is a time of "pilgrimage" – a religious journey. Many Indians who live in the villages still hold some of the beliefs of the Inca peoples who were defeated by the Spanish in the 1500s. The Peruvian Indians feel awe for the great snow-covered peaks of the Andes. They honor the mountains, and they feel that the mountain spirits, or *apus*, have power over their lives.

Christians now take part in

Thousands of pilgrims come to the Qoyllur Rit'i festival from all over southern Peru. Some of them are farmers, others are from the cities.

this journey too. They believe that in 1780 Jesus Christ Himself paid a visit to the Ausangate mountain. There is a chapel on the slopes of the

Peruvians from villages in the Andes think that the mountain peaks are holy places.

mountain. Inside is a painting of Jesus on a rock. People come to worship Jesus, or "the Lord of Qoyllur Rit'i." Many pilgrims carry crosses like the one on

Some of the pilgrims at Qoyllur Rit'i have walked for weeks to be at the festival. They carry their flutes, pipes, and drums with them, dancing as they go.

which Jesus died. There are dancers in colorful costumes and brass bands. Men dress in woolen masks and tunics. They are called *ukukus*, or bear dancers. Early one morning during the festival they carry the crosses onto the snows of the peak. They want the blessing of the mountain apu.

Q'ero Indian tribes believe they are the only true children

It is bitterly cold on the mountainside. Woolen hats, scarves, and thick tunics help the pilgrims keep warm.

of the Incas. They live in their own villages, apart from other Peruvians. They have their own festival at Qoyllur Rit'i. They cut ice from the side of the mountain and carry it back to their villages.

CORPUS CHRISTI

Statues of saints and of Mary, the mother of Jesus, are paraded through Cuzco in this Catholic festival. It is usually held in June.

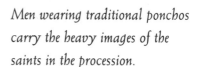

Corpus Christi honors Jesus as well as the Christian sacrament of Holy Communion. Christians receive this sacrament to recall Jesus's death.

People celebrate Corpus Christi with music, dancing, and eating in many parts of Peru. In Cuzco people come to the Plaza de Armas, a square in the city center, which is the heart of the party. The air is full of their talk,

Men wearing traditional ponchos carry the heavy images of the saints in the procession.

the smell of food, and music made by brass bands. There are so many people that you can hardly move.

On the night before the festival people from churches in the area around Cuzco bring in twelve large statues of the Catholic saints and one of Mary, the mother of

Cuzco hosts the best Corpus Christi party. People come from villages miles away to join in the fun. They dress in their best and brightest clothes — often in the traditional colors of their village.

Jesus. On Corpus Christi they carry the statues around Cuzco's Plaza de Armas and into the cathedral. The statues stand on

rite of Holy Communion. Catholics believe that the bread is the same as the body of Jesus Christ, the Messiah.

The music stops when the statues are inside the Cathedral, and people light candles. The statues of the saints and of Mary are left inside the Cathedral overnight. It is believed that the statues talk during the night. Once a rip was found in Mary's dress. People said it was caused by the boot of Saint James. Mary and Saint James danced, they said, on the night of Corpus Christi.

long logs. Men carry them on their shoulders. The men stagger because the statues are so heavy. A brass band marches before each statue.

At the front of the procession is a large float. A silver cup sits on the float. Inside is the bread used in the

Street stalls sell fresh food to the crowds that pack Cuzco. A special dish for Corpus Christi is chiriuchu, *a stew made with corn, guinea pig, and chicken.*

INTI RAYMI

*Actors perform a show based
on the old Inca Festival of the Sun on June 24.
The festival was held by Peruvians long before
the Spanish arrived in Peru in the 1500s.
Today thousands of tourists watch it.*

*Musicians play
flutes and drums covered
with lambs' skin. Dancers in
woven costumes perform as part
of the offering to the Sun.*

In Cuzco on June 24 the people hurry to the old lnca fort of Sacsayhuaman, just over a mile from the city. They pay to sit in a grandstand, or they perch on the ruins of the fort. Then they wait for the Inti Raymi festival to start.

Back in Cuzco an actor dressed in robes and a crown with feathers starts on the journey to the fort. He is the *Inca*, the ruler of the Inca empire. He sits on a throne

*The old Inti Raymi festival lasted
several days. Some people wore
glittering gold costumes. Others
dressed in animal skins and the
feathers of the condor, a bird.
They chanted prayers to the Sun.*

and is carried on the shoulders of men dressed as the royal servants. The men are normally soldiers from the Peruvian army. Some people follow the Inca all the way to Sacsayhuaman. He starts from the Church of Santo Domingo, where the Inca Temple of the Sun once stood. At the Plaza del Cabildo the Inca will make a speech to remind all politicians that they must rule well. Then he goes on to the fort, where the main show takes place.

The Inca starts the performance. A fire is

lighted. It stands for the fires of the Inca empire. Next, priests take hold of a llama.

In the old Inti Raymi festival a priest killed a black llama. He placed it with its head to the east and cut it open. Then he looked at its heart. The people thought that the priest could see the future there. The animal was killed to honor the sun god. But its blood was poured out for Mother Earth. Today the priests pretend to look inside the llama. People cheer when the priests announce that a good year lies ahead.

The actors greet the sun. In the old Inti Raymi

As part of Inti Raymi, priests pretend to kill a llama. In the old festival the llama really was killed. The priest offered the animal to Inti, the Inca god of the Sun.

the people would wait with the Inca for the sun to rise. They would cheer when the sun came up and pray to it all day. The Inca would offer the sun a sip of *chicha*, a drink made from corn.

Inti Raymi is the last day in a party that goes on for a week. It marks the "winter solstice," the shortest day in winter. It is the day on which people begin to look forward to the next summer.

More than 500 actors take part in the show, as soldiers or men and women of the Inca court. Many wear costumes, helmets, and headdresses decorated with dazzling patterns and colorful feathers.

21

MAKE A CROWN

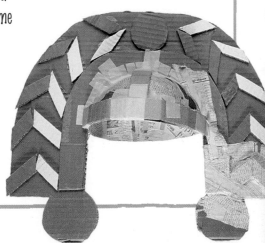

The Peruvian Indians who lived under the Inca rulers in the 1400s believed that one day the Sun would go away. Then they would be unable to grow their crops, and they would starve. The Inti Raymi festival took place in the middle of the Peruvian winter, when there was little sunlight, and the days were the shortest of the whole year. At the festival the Indians prayed for the sun to come back. Sun images are part of the outfits worn by the actors who put on the old festival today. They wear beautiful royal helmets and crowns based on Inca costumes.

YOU WILL NEED
Balloon
Newspaper strips
White glue
Pin
Scissors
Cardboard
Masking tape
White paint
Gold paint
Colored poster paints

1 Choose and blow up a balloon. Cover the balloon with strips of newspaper, using glue. When the paper shell has dried (below left), use a pin to pop the balloon. Remove the balloon from the shell. Cut the paper shell into a helmet shape to fit your head. Next cut out a semicircle of cardboard around the helmet to make a crest for the helmet. Cut some chevrons and circles of cardboard, and stick them onto the crest with glue.

2 Stick the crest onto the helmet with masking tape (below). Cover with strips of newspaper. When it has dried, paint with white paint. Decorate with gold paint and colored poster paints (above).

CONIRAYA AND CAVILLACA

Peruvian legends tell how a race of sun gods once came to Earth to help people. One of the gods, Coniraya, fell in love with a goddess, but she fled from him. As he followed her, he met birds and animals. He blessed the ones that helped him and cursed the others.

CONIRAYA was a sun god, but he dressed in ragged clothes. When he fell in love with a goddess named Cavillaca, she did not want to know him. He gave her a fruit that made her have a baby. Cavillaca fled with her baby son.

Coniraya set out to find her. He met a condor, a large bird like an eagle. The condor said that Cavillaca was heading for the coast. Coniraya gave the condor the gift of strong wings. Next he met a fox, who would not help him. Coniraya told the fox that people would always hate him. He met some parrots, but they would not help him either. Coniraya gave them a loud squawk for a voice. A lion helped him. Coniraya told the lion it would always be honored by people.

When he caught up with Cavillaca and the baby, Coniraya wept. They had turned into stone. But the animals kept the qualities that the sun god had given them.

ILLAPU

People on Taquile Island, on Lake Titicaca in southern Peru, hold musical parties in the summer. Illapu honors the god of thunder.

The people of Taquile Island are famous for their skill as weavers. They wear their finest clothes for Illapu and other parties during the summer.

The celebrations at the Illapu festival go on for seven days. People share bottles of a strong liquor made from sugar cane.

Musical bands provide a strong rhythm for the dancers at Illapu. On the seventh day of the festival all the bands play together.

Women wear skirts with up to 16 layers and brightly colored shawls. The skirts are very precious. When mothers grow old they give their best dresses to their daughters. The men wear tall hats that have been built up with feathers. This is an old custom. Hats like these were worn by men of the Inca tribes in the 1500s.

Weaving is a family business on Taquile Island. Mothers teach their daughters to weave belts. Fathers teach their sons how to make *chullos*, or knitted hats. Each boy has to learn to make his own chullo by the time he is around seven years old. The colors and pictures in the hats have special meanings. Unmarried men wear chullos with white peaks. Married men wear chullos made in bright colors.

The pictures and shapes in the weavers' designs all have a meaning. This flower comes from a retablo, a box with carved scenes inside.

AGUACERO

A - gua - ce - ro de la sie - rra, no me mo - jes mi pon - chi - to

mi - ra que soy pob - re - ci - to y no ten - go mas que uni - to.

Aguacero is a folk song about being caught out in a summer shower.

Rain of the mountain, don't wet my little poncho,
Because I am poor man and I only have this one.

DIA DEL PUNO

Actors dress up to tell the story of the first Inca royal family on November 5. The performance takes place on barges floating on Lake Titicaca, in southern Peru.

The Incas ruled Peru before the Spanish came to the country in 1532. The Inca people had more than one story about the birth of their first kings and queens. One legend tells how the first Inca rulers, Manco Capac and Mama Occlo, were the children of the Sun. They were sent to Earth to help people. The place where they came to Earth was the Island of the Sun, on Lake Titicaca. Some tales say that they came from the lake waters.

A colorful drama retells the story of the

Peruvians wear derby hats on festival days and in their everyday outfits. Derbies became popular in Peru in the 1800s. A British firm found it had made too many hats to sell in Europe. The firm let the hats go at low prices in South America.

People living on Lake Titicaca have to compete with flamingoes and other birds for fish. Fishermen make their own boats from local reeds. The water is over 12,000 feet higher than the sea. It is very cold.

birth of Manco Capac and Mama Occlo. On a brightly decorated barge two people in Indian costume play the roles of the first Inca rulers. Crowds watch from the shore.

Afterward the Inca rulers take part in a procession through the streets of Puno, on the western shore of Lake Titicaca. Groups of musicians in knitted hats and ponchos lead the way. There are many dancers. Some do the *diablada*, or devil dance, which is also an attraction at the Festival of the Virgin of Candelaria held in Puno in February.

For thousands of years Peruvians have seen Lake Titicaca as a holy place. It is easy to

Dancers in the Dia del Puno procession wear their brightest clothes. This manta *is a kind of shawl worn by Peruvian women.*

understand why. The lake is overlooked by mountains of the Andes range. Local fishermen can look at snow-covered peaks while they sit in a boat on the bright blue waters of the lake. Another story about the lake says that in the 1500s the Incas threw all their gold into the lake. They did not want the Spanish to seize the gold.

AGUACATES RELLENOS

MAKES 6

⅔ cup Italian salad dressing
1 tsp mustard
4 large avocados, cut in half and pits removed
½ cup diced cooked green beans
½ cup diced cooked carrots
⅓ cup cooked peas
⅓ cup finely chopped celery
6 pimento-stuffed olives, chopped
2 hard-boiled eggs, shelled and chopped
Salt and pepper
Chopped fresh parsley

1 Put salad dressing in a large bowl. Stir in mustard. Peel one avocado. Put flesh in bowl. Using a fork, mash until blended.
2 Stir in green beans, carrots, peas, celery, olives, and the hard-boiled eggs. Add salt and pepper to taste.
3 Put remaining 6 avocado halves on plates. Spoon vegetable mixture into middles. Sprinkle with parsley and serve.

MANCO CAPAC AND MAMA OCCLO

One legend tells how Manco Capac and Mama Occlo, the first Inca rulers, were born on Lake Titicaca. Another story tells how Manco Capac built the city of Cuzco in a single day. He stopped the sun moving because he was told he had to finish the city before sunset.

IN THE FIRST royal family of the Incas there were four sisters and also four brothers, including Ayar Manco. Manco chose a place to build a city, with all his sisters. But they found that the wind was too strong. Manco caught the wind and put it inside a fenced area used for llamas.

Now his brother Ayar Sauco liked to feel the wind, so he told Manco he would let him keep the wind tied up only for one day. But Manco had an idea. He climbed a mountain and looped a rope around the sun to prevent it moving. The "day" lasted for months. Manco built a great city. He was called Manco Capac – "the Rich King." He married his sister Mama Occlo, and together they ruled the Inca empire.

WEAVE A BAG

Peruvians value skill in weaving very highly. The Q'ero Indians say they are the only true children of the Incas who ruled Peru before the Spanish landed in the 1500s. The Q'eros do not write down words at all. But they use patterns in their weaving. Many of the patterns stand for things, and people know what they mean. It is a kind of writing.

YOU WILL NEED

Picture frame
Hammer
½-inch tacks
Yarn
3-inch sewing needle
Scissors

1 Take a picture frame about 12 inches long by 9 inches wide. Knock 20 tacks into each short end, with about one-fifth of an inch between them. Stretch yarn across the length of the frame, looping it around the tacks. Thread yarn into the sewing needle, and weave in and out between the lengths of yarn on the frame (left).

2 Weave a strip of material about 6 inches long. To change color, cut off one length of yarn in the middle of the frame and then overlap with the new color for the whole width of the material. When you have finished, cut the piece free (left) and tie the loose ends.

3 Double material over and sew up sides to make small bag. Braid pieces of yarn to make a handle for the bag (above). To finish bag, sew on handle (below).

29

MUSICAL INSTRUMENTS

Music and dancing are the main attraction at Peruvian festivals. The musicians play panpipes and stringed instruments like small guitars and violins – as well as trumpets and drums.

Panpipes vary in length from about 5 inches to 5 feet. The longer ones play deeper notes.

Some of the musical instruments in Peru have hardly changed for hundreds of years. Before the Spanish arrived in the 1500s there were no guitars or violins in Peru. But people had panpipes, whistles, flutes, and drums.

Panpipes were well known 2,000 years ago in Greece. The Greeks believed that Pan, their god of hunters and shepherds, invented the instrument. It became known as the "panpipes." When you blow across the top of the pipes, a musical note sounds. Try blowing across the top of an empty bottle. The panpipes work in the same way.

Before the Spanish arrived, Peruvians had their own style of music. Some people still play it today. Americans and Europeans are not used to this music — some find it too harsh. The dance music played at Peruvian festivals today is more like the music Americans and Europeans are accustomed to hearing. Trumpets and other brass instruments play the tune, and drums beat loudly. Panpipes often play the quieter passages.

This type of clay whistle is called an ocarina. Some of these whistles have holes in the shape of a human face on one side (top).

The charango is like a guitar but is much smaller and has a deeper box behind the strings. Peruvian Indians made their own type of guitar, different in style from the Spanish one.

WORDS TO KNOW

Apus: Mountain spirits that were worshiped by the Incas.

Chapel: A small house of worship, either standing on its own or connected to a church.

Conquistadors: The Spanish soldiers who conquered much of South America in the 1600s.

Corpus Christi: A Roman Catholic festival held to honor the sacrament of Holy Communion.

Holy Communion: A Christian ritual that uses bread and wine to commemorate the Last Supper of Jesus Christ.

Holy Week: The week before Easter when Christians commemorate the last days of Christ's life.

Incas: A people who ruled a large South American empire from the twelfth to the sixteenth centuries. Their capital was Cuzco in present-day Peru.

Pachamama: "Mother Earth" in the ancient Inca religion.

Pilgrim: A person who makes a religious journey, or pilgrimage, to a holy place.

Poncho: A traditional Peruvian garment. A poncho is a blanketlike cloak with a hole in the middle for the head.

Roman Catholic: A member of the Roman Catholic Church, the largest branch of Christianity. The head of this church is the pope.

Sacrament: The most sacred type of Christian ritual. Christians believe that the sacraments were started by Jesus Christ. The Roman Catholic Church has seven sacraments.

Saint: A title given to very holy people by some Christian churches. Saints are important in the Roman Catholic Church.

ACKNOWLEDGMENTS

WITH THANKS TO:

Christian Aid, London. Judith Condor, Oxford. Alvaro Graña, teacher and musician, Coventry. The Magic Stone Company, London. The Peru Support Group, London. Embassy of Peru, London. Tumi Ltd., Importers of Latin American Crafts, London and Bath. Vale Antiques, London.

ARTEFACTS BY:

Clay artefacts made by hand in village of Quinua, near Ayacucho, Peru, Tumi Ltd. p6BL, p16BR, p24TR, p26TR.

Details from arpilleras made by Artesiana Peruana Mujeres Creativas, Peru, Christian Aid p11BL, p16-17TL/TR, p19BR.
Details from retablos, made by Joaquin Lopez & Sons, Lima, Peru, Tumi Ltd.p12 BL, p24BL, p25TR.
Hats knitted by women in the area around Juliaca, near Lake Titicaca, Peru, Tumi Ltd. p3, p12TR, p13TL, p17 MR.
Musical instruments made in the workshop of Pablo Quilla, Huancané, Peru, Tumi Ltd. p13BL and BR, p17 Bl, p30 BL.

PHOTOGRAPHS BY:

All photographs by Bruce Mackie except:
John Elliott p11(top).
Cover photograph Pictor International.

ILLUSTRATIONS BY:

Fiona Saunders title page, p4-5, Mountain High Maps ® Copyright © Digital Wisdom, Inc. p4-5. Tracy Rich p7. Robert Shadbolt p23. Josephine Martin p28.

SET CONTENTS